How to Travel Faster Than Light

&

How to Destroy A Dwarf Star

ISBN: 978-1-4717-2580-7

WWW.LULU.COM/SPOTLIGHT/ALANGARFOOT

Cosmic Destiny: The Situation At Hand

The night sky as you may have noticed contains a new member to our solar family called Naberiou, classified as a Brown Dwarf Star. This is a comprehensive essay on what this new solar planetoid spells for planet Earth and the Human race and how we, with what little time we have left, can respond to the threat that this new Dwarf Star poses. This work is not just an outlay of the technology through which a Brown Dwarf or Black hole may be destroyed but also forms a part of the fundamental foundations of interstellar travel. This is not an essay on psycho-spiritual matters of pseudo-science: it focuses specifically on technological solutions to a physical and real cosmic threat which has the potential to cause an Extinction Level Event (ELE).

The Scale of the Crisis: Heat-Stars

As a part of the vast cosmos there are many different interstellar objects on a number of different scales from the very large in the macrocosmic picture such as galaxies and galaxy clusters to those at the very small microcosmic scale such as comets and meteorites. The three scales of cosmic manifestation that concern us here are Gas Giants like Jupiter or Saturn, Stars like Solaris or those of the Pleiadian cluster and Dwarf Stars like the relatively recently discovered Naberiou.

Brown Dwarf Stars in their scale and causal manifest constitution are half way between a Star (which has more mass) and a Gas Giant (which has less mass) With a Brown Dwarf star there is enough nuclear fusion within the planetoid to create heat but not as such enough fusion to create light, which requires more gravity. This extra gravity requires lots more mass making stars proportionally greater in scale then either solid or gaseous planets, so as creating heat and light on a larger scale through having more pressure in and around the core. Due to this lack of light but presence of heat emissions coming from the Dwarf Star it wasn't discovered until NASA put its infra-red telescope in orbit around the earth in 2007.

Unfortunately for us this Dwarf Star lies in an orbit which brings it particularly close to the orbit of our planet earth, close enough to alter the 'green boundary' of heat which is also relevant to Earth's distance from the sun. This 'green boundary' is where planets are positioned close enough to be warm enough, but not too close as to be too hot, or too far away as to be too cold, for planets within this boundary to be potentially life sustaining. If this belt moves due to the extra heat emitted from the Sol orbiting Dwarf Star then earths environment will alter becoming too hot for surface-level life-forms and become inhospitable (ever wondered why Mars looks the way it does?).

Propulsion: Moving Faster Than Light

In order to destroy a planetoid of the scale of Naberiou it is essential that the two following properties being payload (how big the explosion is) and propulsion (how fast the detonating payload is moving at when it detonates) are of such a correlationary nature that when considered as combined together we may actually be able, with this technology, to have a significant effect upon such a scale as to actually be able to influence the orbit or even in all actuality destroy an interstellar object of the Brown Dwarf kind. Propulsion and payload as specific properties have equal causal status, as both properties determine the magnitude of the explosion and also determine what can be realistically destroyed by the weapon system, designed to prevent the Brown Dwarf from coming too close as to eradicate all life.

Electromagnetic Propulsion:

The electromagnetic drive is relatively straightforward, it simply consists of two electromagnets one of lesser and one of stronger field strength. The two magnets are aligned so that when both electromagnets are switched on there is a flow of attraction from the lesser of the magnets to the greater. The trick here is how to transfer this momentum from the electromagnets attraction to each other to the hull of the ship or craft thus creating motion in a direction of travel.

In order for the generated momentum to be transferred both of the magnets at their reverse ends are attached to high tension coiled springs, which are then themselves attached at their reverse ends to the drive container which by a system of concentric rings which then connects to the hull of the vessel. This creates a system where the direction of the ship or crafts movement is determined by the direction that this drive container centrally positioned within the craft is pointing. A variant of this type of propulsion system is to replace the weaker of the two magnets for a spherical vesicle containing a liquid metal (such as Mercury) and letting its attraction to the stronger magnet being responsible for the momentum and motion of the craft or vessel.

All this having been said it is all well and good for us to have the technological capacity to travel at such ridiculous speeds (the sort of speed necessary to destroy a Brown Dwarf) but what is the point if what we are transporting, when we approach or are at speeds faster then light, cant take the extreme forces experienced at those speeds and ends up being simply torn apart? The answer is to reduce or if possible completely cancel out the inertia and hence the momentum of transport propulsion so as that the contents be it technology or people can move at those speeds without being ripped limb from limb or being completely torn apart. What here is needed in order for faster than light travel is an inertial dampening field.

Hyperspatial Travel & The Inertial Dampening Field:

Inertia as a quality of reality or property of the manifest universe is I believe best described as realities fundamental and innate central tendency to typically resist physical force or manifest movement as considered as of being outside of any reasonable field of gravity. Weight as such is a sub-property of the mass of an object which manifests from mass when it is placed within a gravity, here however it is not the weight of an object but its mass which resists the physical force exerted upon it and hence forms what we know as the universal property of inertia.

In order to explain the nature of inertia it is necessary that we first take stock of a few fundamental assumptions about the laws of physics and the nature of reality. The core assumptions and dynamics being considered are those of hyperspatial displacement, zero-point energy harmonics and a comprehension of the roperty of inertia and momentum as a polemic duality of a manifest elastic eather (hyperspace) at the zero-point level.

In the moment at the point of the big bang we see the explosion of the four dimensions of spacetime into existence in the form of energy and matter. But what we also see at the moment of the big bang is the contraction of the remaining six dimensions of hyperspace. These dimensions contracted into a quasi-existence of energetic form so as to create an intricate mesh of sub-nanoscopic transdimensional doughnuts interlinked through energetic harmonisation at the hyperspatial level. One of the energetic manifest properties of the [objective] dimensionalisation of hyperspatial reality is the manifestation of the [subjective] energy dynamics of the manifest universe, such as inertia.

Energy dynamics such as the transmission and movement of light, gravity, magnetism as packets of energy quanta using the zero-point hyperspatial energy eather as a means of manifestation and movement. But also it can be said that the hyperspatial eather being so fundamental to the nature of the manifest universe and the dimensions of physical reality, that at weaved at the fundamental level of the atomic vibration of a superstring, we see that the natures of both strong nuclear and electroweak nuclear force are also dependant for their physical manifestation upon the multidimensional eather.

The energy dynamic that we will most fundamentally concerned with here in this consideration of hyperspace and its many qualities is the [subjective] physically manifest causal dynamic of the momentum/inertia energy duality. Ultimately this duality is a single force that we shall soon see is essentially the determination of a force which is so hyperspatially dependent for its physical tangibility, its movement and its causal force that if the lower dimensional hyperspatial eather is displaced at a particular frequency then the path of a photon (light quanta) will follow this displacement as if nothing was in any way abnormal or different with the whole affair.

The hyperspatial eather is in its essential nature a quasi-dimensional energy matrix connecting the realms of immiscible higher dimensional doughnut shaped zero-point electromagnetic tension rings to be connected through a nexus of manifestation to the lower physically manifest dimensions of spacetime through the dynamics of hyperspace. Through the doughnuts higher-dimensional contraction we see the lower dimensional emergence of the hyperspatial property of inertial locality as an existence made of an essence where the tension converges into a focus found in the centre or the eye of the ring of the doughnut shaped hyperspatial contraction as the point of strongest manifestation creating an impression in time-space of hyper-space.

This impression manifests in spacetime as a composite energy-physicality dimensional fundamental constitution which as a nexus of manifestation combines the tension of the higher-dimensions through their penetration in the form of hyperspace of the higher dimensions into the fundamental mechanics of the lower dimensional physical properties of spacetime. This penetration of the higher dimensions into the lower ones creates a fundamental existential property of the physical and material universe whereby an energy is created which obeys the elastic dynamics of the hyperspatial multidimensional eather harmonised into the energetic unity we experience as the inertia/momentum duality.

The ability of hyperspace to penetrate matter whereby creating an elastic inertia/momentum energy dynamic as the creation and product of the vibration of the eather as it resonates with the vibration of the superstring relative to how fast the energy-net of hyperspatial energy moves through the atom whereby creating a quantity. As such it is this interaction at a fundamental level of an elastic hyperspatial eather with the physical causal structures of manifest matter at the zero-point level which makes the displacement of hyperspace possible through the displacement of the fundamental energy dynamic of momentum/inertia.

As such when considering the future of aeronautic technology we soon see that the dynamics of inertia and momentum generated through travelling at great speed as such poses quite a significant problem for the engineers and physicists of our days and times. An example is that when travelling at the incredibly tremendous velocities between cosmic objects like planets, star-systems and even galaxies.

Looking at the intricate math involved in interstellar and interplanetary travel we soon find that for the safe transportation of such delicate, soft and breakable objects as fusion bombs or even one day ourselves, that we need on both a theoretically feasible rationalisation and technologically valid and practical level the creation of what some science-fiction writers call an inertial dampening field. We must essentially create science fact from science fiction in the theoretical schematisation of a technological device whose function would be a close approximation of what I define as a hyperspatial displacement device, a device capable of warping inertia around the vessel, person or craft. This explanation I discussing and speaking of here is not just a chief concern for those seeking a solution to the ominous and looming threat of the Dwarf Heat-Star Naberiou now hanging obvious to all but the ignorant in the night sky.

The hyperspatial displacement device I will come to explain the workings of in a brief moment, after having first considered further the exact nature of hyperspace and the fundamental dichotomy of the essential unified duality of the inertia/momentum polemic of manifest force/counterforce in the energy dynamic of momentum/inertia.

In the theoretical dynamics of the physics of today we find that momentum and inertia is a fundamental concern for all those scholars and scientists who still despite the staunch criticism of their peers believe that interstellar travel even though being beyond the confines and boundaries of the current paradigm may one day to the human race be possible. that they face identify physics with the creative essences of visualisation, conceptualisation and analogy. They are those amongst us in the scientific community who hold a hope in their hearts: the hope that interstellar travel will one day be possible.

I shall now outline a little further my critical theory of how at a fundamental level the energy dynamics of momentum and inertia are essentially the opposite ends of the causal polar dynamics of what is ultimately one single unified energy system. To put another way we shall soon see that inertia and momentum are opposite sides or poles of one and the same fundamental hyperspatially dependent universal energetic force. Seeing these two individuated and opposed polemic dynamics (much like the magnetic poles in the form of North and South or positive and negative electric charge at the subatomic level) are as of such a fundamental nature so as of being at a more fundamental dimensionalisation they are essentially determined in their causal constitution as products of an elastic zero-point hyperspatial eather. The nature of this hyperspatial eather is one which through the correct technological innovation and theoretical application can be either bent, warped or displaced around a person, ship or vessel.

In the new subject area in the sciences and particularly in the realm of Physics of the theory of hyperspatial dynamics we see the qualification of the fundamental mechanics of the universe anew from an inspired and fresh perspective. Entwined within the weave of this new perspective's constitution we find ourselves redefining the exact existential nature of our personally experienced and defined reality again. This realities boundaries and dynamics as we have all our lives previously experienced and understood from the theoretical dynamics and dispositions of our own previous particular individual ideological being constitutes the dynamics which on an individual and sociocultural level form the fundamental dynamics of a paradigm shift considered as a cultural level. It is this being that at the individual and social level becomes metamorphicly transformed in the wake of the synthesis and refinement of the processes and dynamics of the paradigm shift of hyperspatial dynamics which our cosmic destiny depends so very much upon.

As such with the dynamics of hyperspace when considered as of being fundamentally and theoretically based upon and grounded within the theoretical dynamics of the exact causal nature of zero-point energy and hyperspace we see through the practicalisation of the theory in the quantification of the newly qualified hyperspatial dimensions a new paradigm emerge, overcome and transcend the boundaries of the previous.

Also through this practicalisation of the theoretical mechanics of the paradigm of Hyperspatial Dynamics we see through revision and refinement the development and evolution of new technological innovations and designs which attempt to manipulate reality or matter as according to our theoretical explanations and the practical mechanics of the theory we choose to advocate or believe in. Not only are the dimensions of hyperspace explained through the fusion of our creative and imaginative dynamics of mind with those of logic and rationalisation but it also gives us the solution to our negative cataclysmic cosmic world fate; the impending Naberiou crisis.

It also gives the Human Race through both the world powers becoming significantly united in their solution to this cosmic crisis and having been liberated of their dystopian interstellar fate will have also been given the technological keys to our new positive collective social destiny which lies before us as the exploration of the vast interstellar cosmos of the milky way and beyond. Darwin's theories of evolution through the survival of the fittest and the rule of nature only apply if there are limited or scarce resources; if we become an interstellar race and learn to exploit the resources of the universe then surely through nearly limitless resources we can learn to share and co-evolve as socially liberated beings of nearly limitless potential and unique true individuality.

Inertia as such is the causal property or otherwise central law-like tendency of individuated objects of physical matter outside of the immediate causal zone of a field of gravity to resist acceleration or positive motion. As the counterforce we can see the fundamental dynamics of momentum as the central tendency of material manifest objects of the physical universe outside of an immediate field of gravity to resist deceleration or negative motion.

It appears that at a fundamental level when an object is placed within 'constant conjunction' with another such as in when two objects transfer momentum and inertia as casual properties when the two physical objects such as two billiard balls one stationary and one moving collide. In this example we see a crude transmission of physical energy from one object to another as the momentum of the moving ball is transferred with the inertia of the stationary ball; we may not see the literal causality itself but at least on one level we can observe its manifest physical effects.

It is as it appears to me that the inertia acting upon the stationary billiard ball as a potential energy is passed through the causality of the manifest connection of the kinetic energy undergoing dynamic transference through the physical contact between the two billiard balls. The static energy of the stationary ball in this example is transferred through the physical contact from the stationary ball to the moving ball which results momentum of this moving ball previously in motion to come to an abrupt halt through absorbing the static inertia and the energy of the momentum being transferred from the ball in motion to the static ball causing it to move onwards.

In this dynamic of forces seen in the billiard ball example I have just used we see the previously stationary billiard ball, through the dynamic of physical contact, not only transfers an immediate jolt of inertia halting the moving ball but through losing inertia there is a space created within the stationary ball in its place where momentum is absorbed and manifest and the stationary billiard ball therefore moves. This is an example of how inertia and momentum function as a part of a more fundamental dimensional unity in which I believe that within the realms of the higher dimensions the polemic of momentum as 'opposite sides of the same coin' I would analogise that in higher dimensions the two sides are merged in the edge which represents their unity as a ten dimensional hyperspatial unity connecting them; on a fundamental level they would both have and share one unified essence and that one of the dimensions of hyperspace we are immediately aware of not as a property of matter but as a universal higher dimensional hyperspatial energy.

Hyperspace is a theory of a universal energy field permeating and penetrating all matter that can be manipulated through electro-magnetic zero-point energy oscillation. This is done through feeding a alternating current through an electro-magnet which should alternate at the same frequencies that hyperspace vibrates at the electromagnetic level. Through the patterns being the same consisting of a harmonic of different wavelengths (this can be done through altering the wavelength of the oscillation mid flow to create what I can a waveform) the energy dynamics of the magnets and hyperspace displace each other and through the electromagnetic manipulation of the fabric of hyperspace results in the photo-electric, infra-red and inertial manipulation of reality around a person or craft.

The displaced hyperspatial zero-point eather desires by its very nature to return to its point of origin as the harmonised focus of higher-dimensional energy in the centre of its doughnut ring at a sub-quantum field causality level of existence where it resides in a state of balanced harmony. Naturally this pressure forces back against the displacer magnets but this manifestation of a force of resistance is not the death of this theory.

If the vessel is of a teardrop or tadpole shape and along the sides of the ship or craft displacer magnets are fitted which oscillate at the same frequency as hyperspace then the pressure of the hyperspatial displacement of the zero-point electromagnetic eather regaining locality should propel the ship onwards. Yet it can be said that with hyperspace being tensile exerts physical force and therefore the faster we go the more hyperspace we encounter and the quicker it needs displacing: the stronger the displacer magnets at the fore of the craft need to be to meet this displacement demand. This is however assuming that hyperspace exerts a physical cumulative electromagnetic force when compressed or displaced, it could be the case that hyperspace exhibits when manipulated no such manifest tendencies and that all the dimensionalisations of force, mass and weight are properties of the lower physical dimensions of spacetime and have no governance in the dimensionalisation and essential natures of hyperspace.

Warp Pulse-Wave Propulsion:

This form of propulsion system is based ultimately on one principle which all propulsion systems have in common with each other: displacement. This is true whether it be the turbine in a jet engine or the propeller of a modern boat; be it the displacement of the medium of air, water, or in this case: hyperspace.

The idea is that if you have a tensor magnet vibrating at the frequency of hyperspace then the vibration of which we are speaking creates a pinch or a tension in the multidimensional hyperspatial eather. A motion may be introduced to the workings of the system by having other magnets spinning at the poles in the same direction as each other which would create pulses of tensile eather shooting from one of the poles of the tensor magnet which should in theory create motion as the reaction force of these pulses is the movement of the craft or vessel.

If you have these pulse-wave projectors set into a sphere covering many angles in a variety of arrangements then a ship, craft or vessel could be made very manoeuvrable.

Payload: The Scale of Detonation & The Nova Bomb

With explosives the fundamental principle at either the chemical or physical level is that of creating a rapid chain reaction within the compound or material so as that a lot of energy can be released in a very short space of time. The idea here is of successfully destroying Naberiou and its constellation so as that it does not come so close to planet Earth as to endanger its inhabitants (us!). Within this part of this piece of work it is my intention to explain the dynamics of nuclear cluster fusion in a way so as that this valid and reliable methodological blueprint can be both explained paradigmatically in terms of the culture of science and of plasma physics; but most fundamentally can also be used as a methodological blueprint for the united scientists of the world to create them in the necessary number within the necessary amount of time. In order to destroy a heat star we need something far in excess of anything conventional science civilian or military currently has to offer us; so let us start again from the fundamental principles.

To start with we need positively charged atomic hydrogen (H2) so as that it will magnetically react to and therefore compress if placed between the positive (North) poles of a few strong magnetic fields. This atomic hydrogen we can obtain through the simple reaction of some Magnesium in some Hydrochloric Acid for example, the trick is then compressing it and allowing for it to cool so as to eventually at zero degrees Kelvin as a solid block it can be sealed within a diamond.

Diamonds can take extreme heat and pressure so because of this factor they are ideal for containing the atomic hydrogen. The hydrogen is then super-heated by converging lasers and compressed through converging magnetic fields into a tight dense plasma that when subjected to a neutron burst trigger fuses into helium which further compresses the remaining hydrogen into H3 releasing an even bigger kick and like a wave in a supernova this compresses into further elements releasing enough energy (it is hoped) to destroy a heat star such as Naberiou if launched so as to destroy it in a spiral from the edge inwards so as not to increase the rate of fusion within the Brown Dwarf any further. If fusion can be controlled by the influx of neutrons in a steady flow then modified in a slightly different conceptualisation of the original idea a thruster technology whereby the rate of fusion is controlled by the rate of neutron exposure could easily be realised. The fusion rate of the thruster or payload is of course determined and limited by the amount of energy which can be initially placed within the causal workings of the system so as to provide a large enough kick of energy so as to make it that nuclear fusion can be actually be achieved on the level necessary to destroy a Brown Dwarf heat star.

Zero-Point Power Source & Explosion Scale

The idea of actually achieving perpetual motion is oft scorned at by engineers and physicists alike as at best impossible and worst an in-joke which defines clearly the initiates and the adept in the subject, but it is now my turn to attempt to do something a little differently. Firstly we need to create a self-sustaining system and the only way to do this is reduce the energy loss of the system to zero, then we can look at whether or not it is possible using a modified generator to tap the zero-point hyperspatial electromagnetic eather as a power source.

Due to the higher dimensional unity of inertia/momentum force with electromagnetism motion of a electrically conductive object through a magnetic field with a critical amount of kinetic energy causes electrons to overcome their hyperspatial tethering and come out of compactification where they would otherwise exist embedded within the eather and manifest as electric current. In order to tap the resultant current generated by the magnet as a viable source of electromagnetic energy we place wires in the electromagnetic field of the source magnet so as that as this source magnet rotates in sufficient motion then electrons will manifest in the wire and an electric current will be generated.

To the causal dynamics of the zero-pointy generator I am proposing here there are three prevalent drains on the energy of the system, these are: air pressure/resistance, axial suspension rod friction and the earths magnetic field. The first of these can be solved by sealing the generator in a vacuum so as to reduce the energy lost to air resistance/pressure to zero, this is the first of these energy drains solved.

Next is the friction at either end of the axial suspension rod which is threaded through the width of the central core of the spinning source magnet so as to make it that as the source magnet rotates so too does the suspension rod of the zero-point generator move in accordance with its rotation. In order to reduce the loss of the energy of the system through the causal dynamics of friction at either of the opposite connective ends of the axial suspension rod.

We could use a non water based lubricant such as graphite which due to its nature would give the system a reasonably high rate of energy efficiency but what we need here is 100% efficiency so here we need a bit of innovation to create the desired level of efficiency. What we need is not actually that radical an idea, the bullet train in Japan runs on very similar principles; what we need are floatation magnets at either end of a magnetic axial rod to reduce the energy bleed to zero.

The only other loss of energy within the systems dynamics would be negligible in effect here on Earth but in the core of a Dwarf Star or Black Hole would be vastly stronger and would have an effect upon the functioning of the zero point generator. Therefore a very strong Faraday Cage would have to exist between the functional zone of the generator and the magnetic field of the Dwarf Star or Black Hole's core so as to negate its effect with an electromagnetic barrier shield. Essentially what we now have is a self-sustaining system, but can we turn it into something more?

The filaments of the uptake wires of the generator come in two types; those which supply energy to a further system or subsystem and those which feed back into the system to sustain it. In order to create an increasingly faster rate of rotation of the source magnet then electromagnets designed to attract and repel are sequenced in such a way as to create circular motion of the generator magnet at increasingly faster speeds. These electromagnets have their own separate uptake filaments in the magnetic field of the source magnet designed to keep the system to a constant level of electromagnetic saturation which the main uptake wires take as the output of the system.

Conclusion: The Fate of the Human Race?

The very real situation and challenge forced upon us by the greater cosmic macrocosm of the universe is that we either unify and overcome this cosmic dilemma or we break apart, fail and face the ultimate final curtain of an Extinction-Level-Event. We have the potential within the capabilities of our minds, selves and also of our higher nature as we can develop through introspection that we can become a space-faring, emancipated, liberated race of positively empowered and culturally rich, diverse and learned individuals. All of the human race unified, equal and inspired of the lived ideas and values which define our self, autonomy and ideology as understood as of being at a fundamental level composed of different causal dynamics of the manifest subconscious will. I dream of the joy of being a part of an emancipated space-fairing race of what potentially could be countless thousands of successfully colonised worlds in our Galaxy the Milky Way and beyond, this as such would be the utopian vision for humanities future and is my hope as well that the potential higher nature of humanity comes to fruition.

The fundamental reason why I have written this piece of work is essentially change the fate of the Human race, so that instead of perishing in the savage and barren environment of a cosmically originated apocalyptic & dystrophic end we can instead destroy the heat star then united as one we can go and colonise other worlds and become a race of the stars, a truly glorious destiny I believe. Instead of an alien race coming here and treating us like savage subordinates and inferiors we can go to the stars and meet them as space faring united equals.

Instead of a downwards spiral of self destruction as our collective social destiny we will in fact face and overcome this negative fate. Instead through the creative processes and logical abilities unique on Earth to the Human Race we will analyse, synthesise, harmonise and ultimately unify on both the political, cultural and political level on a global scale. Through this shift in the tangent of our collective destiny where together through facing and overcoming the dystopian cosmic destiny through averting this potential disaster and through becoming a space faring species we may ultimately achieve for the benefit and enjoyment of the future generations a level of personal, social, scientific and cultural enlightenment never before previously imagined by us ourselves or our distant ancestors of all the many civilisations who have come before us.

www.ingramcontent.com/pod-product-compliance
Lightning Source LLC
Chambersburg PA
CBHW031142270326
41931CB00007B/660